*Quick*GUIDES

everything you need to know...fast

Fundraising From Wealthy Individuals

by Julian Smyth

reviewed by Frank Opray

WIREMILL
PUBLISHING LTD

Across the world the organizations and institutions that fundraise to finance their work are referred to in many different ways. They are charities, non-profits or not-for-profit organizations, non-governmental organizations (NGOs), voluntary organizations, academic institutions, agencies, etc. For ease of reading, we have used the term Nonprofit Organization, Organization or NPO as an umbrella term throughout the *Quick*Guide series. We have also used the spellings and punctuation used by the author.

Published by
Wiremill Publishing Ltd.
Edenbridge, Kent TN8 5PS, UK
info@wiremillpublishing.com
www.wiremillpublishing.com
www.quickguidesonline.com

British Library Cataloguing in Publication Data
A catalogue record for this book is available from the British Library.

ISBN Number 1-905053-04-5

Printed by Rhythm Consolidated Berhad, Malaysia
Cover Design by Jennie de Lima and Edward Way
Design by Colin Woodman Design

CONTENTS

**FUNDRAISING FROM
WEALTHY INDIVIDUALS**

Fundraising from wealthy individuals is probably the least understood element in the fundraising mix, which is probably why it is undertaken so infrequently by so many nonprofit organisations (NPOs). And yet any organisation can successfully fundraise from wealthy individuals. Indeed, some of the most successful are organisations with few members of staff and without large budgets for special events, direct marketing to large numbers of people or a high public profile.

So what are the main differences between fundraising from those individuals with high net worth and the remainder of the population?

Major donors are less interested in your agenda than they are in their own. You need to find empathy between what is important to them and what you are looking to achieve.

Whereas in conventional fundraising one is looking to *communicate* a message, in major-gift fundraising one must cultivate the art of *listening* to the donor.

Wealthy individuals very rarely give large sums of money for unrestricted use – they are project-driven and need to be approached in that vein.

Soliciting support from this constituency *always* requires a face-to-face approach, and most often not by a professional fundraiser but by a senior volunteer (often with professional support).

NPOs looking to garner support from these individuals must be willing to give up far more than just their time to secure the gifts. Wealthy individuals desire participation in the projects or services they are funding and often wish to have hands-on involvement.

Your organisation's gift stewardship policy must be set in stone before any wealthy individuals are approached. What thanking procedures do you have in place? What are you willing to offer in return for a substantial gift? Can the donor name (or rename) the project or service he or she is funding?

INTRODUCTION

Major gifts take much longer to secure. A period of one to three years from initial contact to successful solicitation is not at all uncommon, and research has shown that the largest gifts often come between 11 and 13 years after the donor begins to become involved.

Major gifts from individuals are more often made from capital than from income. They are not, therefore, likely to be annual events.

Fundraising from wealthy individuals is a matter of both whom you know *and* what you know. To be successful you must employ a sustained and logical process of developing the prospective donor from total stranger to lifelong friend – in other words, *moves management*.

This process can be codified and logically explained, as follows:

- Researching
- Connections
- Friend-raising
- Communicating
- Approaching
- Soliciting
- Stewardship and involvement

The following chapters will take you through each stage, leading to:

"The right person asking the right person for the right thing at the right time for the right amount"

Research, conventional fundraising wisdom suggests, should take up 50 percent of a fundraising office's time. In practice, this seldom happens. However, it is still a good target to aim for and will always pay dividends.

Research into wealthy individuals has three main aims:

- To ascertain individuals' capacity to give. Do they have enough money to make it worth your while?

- To ascertain what, if any, connections you can find to allow you to make an initial approach. Does anybody you know also know them?

- To ascertain what, if any, propensity they have to give to you. Do they have a record of supporting similar causes or do they have interests in or family links to what you do?

You are, therefore, looking to find out:

- Their recorded family wealth, business activities, holdings, salary, property, etc.

- Any cross-referencing to other constituents on your database.

- Giving history to other causes (or your own), activities, interests, personal and family biographies, trusteeships of other charities, public pronouncements on causes similar to your own, etc.

This may seem a daunting task when setting out for the first time into the realm of major gifts from individuals, but there is a lot of information you can find from other members of your constituency, publicly available sources and research specialists.

Research firms can provide, usually expensively, profiles of your current supporters. Freelance researchers can do this as well, usually at a fraction of the cost.

There are huge variations in what information is publicly available depending upon the country in which you work. The following will be available in most countries:

- Registers of public companies, showing shareholdings, directors' remuneration, dividend payments, and details of major share sales and purchases.

- Registers of professional bodies (accountants, lawyers, surveyors, etc.).

- "Who's Who"-type publications and published "Rich Lists."

- Searchable CD-ROMs offered for sale by private companies.

- Subscription databases, which can be very expensive but are a gold mine of information.

Two of the most lucrative areas in terms of research, however, cost nothing at all – the Internet and good old-fashioned gossip.

On the Internet, simply type a name into a major search engine and see just how much information is available, including:

- Short biographies of senior staff on companies' Web sites.

- Biographies of speakers at major seminars and conferences.

- Annual reports with directors, shareholders and officers listed.

- Personal or family Web sites, where a wealth of information is often provided.

Don't forget gossip or, more formally, "anecdotal information." Ask around the office as well as conducting more formal screening exercises (where senior volunteers scroll through lists prepared by you to see whom they might know and have information on).

Reviewer's Comment

In my experience, many organisations rely almost exclusively on anecdotal information and ignore the more formal process of identifying relevant information. Both anecdotal and formally researched information are useful.

You will also need to ensure you have a proper, fully relational database for storing the great deal of in-depth information you will procure. Your standard database may not be adequate for this purpose.

Knowing who the wealthy people are is one thing. Finding a connection to your cause is quite another. How do you find a way of standing out from the crowd?

To a certain extent, the very process of researching these individuals should help in this regard. If you uncover the fact that someone's father was deaf and you are working for a deafness-related cause, the connection is self-evident.

Such a fact may, of course, be quite hard to uncover, and the majority of connections are personal ones rather than shared ideals that may only become evident when you begin the process of cultivation. It is very dangerous to be mesmerised by the wealth of an individual and thus pursue a solicitation that is simply never going to happen because you have no way of making that initial connection.

So, what might these connections be? Some examples:

■ Locality – wealthy people like to support causes local to where they live or where they have business premises.

■ Friendships – someone you know knows the prospect.

■ Business – someone you know knows the prospect through business connections.

■ Usage – someone close to the prospect has made use of your services.

■ Company donor – the prospect works for a company that already supports your cause.

■ They have a history of giving to like-minded causes.

The best place to start looking for these connections is among your current senior volunteers and your board. Produce long lists of those whom you have previously identified as being capable of a major gift and then sit down with these volunteers, either singly or in groups, and annotate the lists with the connections you can unearth. Work outwards from the centre to develop your contacts.

Similarly, look for home and business addresses, not forgetting branch offices and subsidiaries, and research giving histories for similar causes to your own.

Use your relational database to track links to the prospect's career history to identify whether the prospect works for or has worked for or owns companies that are donors to your organisation.

Finally, use a simple two-part code to categorise these prospects. If, for example, A to E signifies how wealthy they are (A being wealthiest) and 1 to 5 signifies how warm they are to your cause (1 being warmest), then it is clear that more time should be spent immediately on the A1s than the E5s. Similarly, extra effort should be employed to move the A5s toward A1 status. In this way, you can track your developing relationship with these prospective donors.

Identifying the right prospects and moving them from someone unknown to your organisation to being a lifelong supporter is the goal.

FRIEND-RAISING

It is an old adage of fundraising that friend-raising comes before fundraising, and this is never so true as when soliciting wealthy individuals.

Friend-raising activities are not fundraising activities. They are opportunities to inform strangers about what and who you are, what good work you do, how much you are willing to listen as well as talk, and what the defined need is for your organisation.

People are naturally wary of any invitations that come out of the blue, so occasions you organise must not be camouflaged fundraising events. Once it becomes clear that you will not be asking the invitees to give, the atmosphere becomes much more constructive and the guests start taking a real interest in what you might be saying to them.

By far the most effective friend-raising opportunities are not, as one might suppose, grand charity balls or tickets for major sporting events. They are opportunities to see your organisation being effective at whatever it does. That is not to say that private briefing sessions will not be required, but if you want to "sell" your organisation, then the prospective donor has to see it in action.

Consider some of the following:

■ Open days wherein you have a separate and accompanied major prospect "track".

■ Private visits to your facilities or operation.

■ Site visits to new projects under construction.

■ Meetings open to the public.

■ Hands-on interactive events, such as career fairs in educational institutions.

■ Any events that bring your prospects face-to-face with the beneficiaries of your charitable work.

You need to show your work with no hint of "stage management" but equally should give your prospective major donors special treatment within such opportunities. Ensure that there are members of staff (the more senior the better) available to answer questions, explain what the guests are seeing, and subtly get the message across of your success and your ongoing needs. Food and drink should be appropriate for the occasion. Attention to detail is a prerequisite to success.

Peer-to-peer relationships and networking are important at friend-raising events. The prospective donor's confidence in your organisation often comes from the fact that he or she recognises others (at least by reputation) who are also attending such events.

Face-to-face meetings in the early part of a relationship-building exercise are also friend-raising opportunities and not merely solicitation exercises.

Finally, keep in your mind at all times that all friend-raising opportunities are two-way streets. It is not simply a matter of informing the prospects of what wonderful people you are and what wonderful work you do. You must at all times be *listening* and learning everything you can about the way the prospect thinks and feels.

He or she is unlikely to put a large amount of money into something with which he or she has no empathy. Before you begin to think about an approach for a major donation, you need to find out what the prospect is more likely to support. Does he or she prefer capital, revenue or endowment projects? Is the work you do with young children going to be a more fruitful area for development than the work you do with adults? In other words, what is likely to be on the prospective donor's agenda rather than yours?

Reviewer's Comment
The concept of the "hot button" is worthwhile to introduce at this point. My experience is that people new to the fundraising arena relate well to the idea of seeking to uncover the potential donor's "hot button," which is the thing that really interests him or her.

Once meetings and events are over, run debriefing sessions with your staff and volunteers. Collate all the information uncovered and make sure it is entered into your database for later use.

Aim to communicate with your potential major prospects at least 12 times per year. Indeed, it is arguable that all of your current and potential supporters should hear from you this often.

What this does *not* mean, however, is that you should be sending 12 pieces of appeal literature every year. Communication is how you keep yourself in the mind of your major gift prospect. He/she needs to know that yours is a dynamic organisation, that things are going well (people give to secure the continuation of success, not to stave off disaster in your organisation), and that you are treating him/her as an individual and not just a number or an open wallet.

You must also take into consideration the bald fact of life that much direct mail is simply not read. With even the best of intentions, many of us simply never get around to opening the newsletter, reading the briefing paper or studying the annual report. You therefore need to adopt a "drip drip" approach – keep on reiterating the message you wish to put across in as many different and varied ways as possible.

The more personal such communications can be, the better, and do not be afraid to be adventurous in how you choose to stay in contact. Here are some examples:

- Newsletters – these should be interesting, informative, easy to read and digest, full of colour photographs illustrating your work or the achievements of those you have helped.

- Annual reports – again, these should not be staid documents but accessible, informative and as informal as regulations allow.

- Interim or "draft" reports showing that the prospect is getting information in advance of the rank and file.

- Christmas cards.

- Birthday cards.

- Additional thank-you letters at the end of the financial year setting out how much they have donated in the previous year, for tax purposes.

- "Catch-up" letters keeping the prospect informed and up to date on developments relating to previous discussions.

- Invitations to events, open days, annual general meetings, etc.

- Follow-up letters to events that the prospect has attended, thanking him/her for coming.

- "Draft" documents (especially Cases for Support) asking for comments and opinions before they are published.

- Annual fund literature.

It is not difficult to arrive at 12 communications utilising only some of the above. If cost is a major issue, then consider the use of e-mail and the Web to reduce print bills (produce the newsletter or annual report on your Web site, for example, and then merely e-mail the prospect to tell him/her where to find this information). Indeed, there is much to be said for e-mails because, unlike information sent through the mail and telephone calls, they tend to go directly to the prospect rather than be filtered through secretaries and executive assistants.

Consider writing all envelopes to major donor prospects by hand rather than trusting them to automated mail-sort programmes, and perhaps add a little personal note (on a postcard or a compliment slip) to a mass-produced communication such as a newsletter. Always open and close letters by hand and consider who should be writing to the prospective major donor. Perhaps the chief executive or chairman of the board is a better person than the fundraising director?

Reviewer's Comment
You need to do what is appropriate in your country. Topping and tailing letters means writing by hand "Dear John" and "Yours sincerely" and is used to demonstrate a more personal relationship between the writer and recipient. If there is something else that would demonstrate a personal approach in your country, you should consider doing that.

The actual solicitation of a major gift must, of course, begin with an approach for a meeting. If all of the activities as set out in the previous chapters have been followed, then this may not be a major issue. The prospect is such a good friend of yours by now that a simple telephone call will set up the appointment.

In reality, of course, things are seldom quite that simple. The obtaining of a private appointment during which the actual solicitation is made can be fraught with problems. By the very nature of their wealth, major donor prospects can be very difficult to get hold of and have all sorts of barriers designed to keep them from being bothered by the many people who want some of their time.

There are, therefore, a number of hurdles to be gone through, and planning is essential. First of all, who should make the approach? Try the following in descending order:

■ The best person is someone known to the prospect, someone who has himself/herself made a major donation – in other words, a peer-to-peer approach is best.

■ If this person is unwilling to do the actual asking, he or she may nevertheless be willing to set up the meeting personally and perhaps attend in an observing capacity.

■ If any direct involvement by the volunteer is not possible, he or she may still be willing to recommend to the prospect, either by letter or phone, that a meeting should be accepted.

■ Finally, if all else fails, then a direct approach by someone from your organisation must be used.

If you are required to undertake the last course of action, here are some "tricks of the trade" you may want to try:

■ If the person you are trying to reach has a secretary who is instructed to obstruct access to the boss, try telephoning the office when the secretary is unlikely to be there – before office hours, during lunch, and after office hours. Successful individuals tend to be workaholics and often work longer hours than their employees.

- Circumvent the office altogether and call the prospect at home. Be careful to ensure that it is at a convenient time and be sure to include the spouse in any suggested meeting.

- Use e-mail – whereas the post and the telephone are the domain of the secretary, most people read and answer their own e-mails.

- Always make some passing reference to previous hospitality that you gave the donor prospect during the "warming" or "friend-raising" phase. It is far more difficult to refuse a meeting when the prospect effectively "owes" you a lunch or a drink.

- Most diaries are organised in half-hour slots, and 30 minutes is not long enough to make an effective solicitation. Equally, an hour may appear too long to the prospect with a very busy schedule. Ask, therefore, for a meeting of about 45 minutes: It won't appear too long but you will almost certainly get the full hour because there will be nothing else in the diary until the next slot.

Achieving a meeting is by no means the end of the matter — the meeting place is equally important. The best venue is definitely either the prospect's office or home, and experience would suggest that the former is more likely to be offered than the latter. The wealthy individual will feel secure and relaxed on familiar ground and in command of the situation. This is important because solicitation must not be a "hard sell" but a decision made by the prospect him or herself, which you are merely facilitating.

The nature of the friend-raising process, however, may well lead the prospect to offer you a lunch or dinner, or to suggest a venue away from the hustle and bustle of the office. This can cause problems in terms of the ambience and practicality of actually "making the ask" in such surroundings.

Imagine, for example, how you would explain the capital project you are looking for the prospect to support, in a wine bar where the table between you is the size of a large dinner plate and is already fully covered with two

Continues on next page

glasses of wine and two plates full of food? In addition, the bar is full of young financial traders celebrating their bonuses with champagne after a good month. There is nowhere to put your explanatory material, your project plans, or your artist's rendering of the finished building; the noise is horrendous; and the prospect is, in any event, wary of saying too much in a place where he or she could be overheard by an acquaintance.

A very different problem might arise in a club or other place that will not allow you to take out papers within the building. Again, if you have no explanatory materials, no forms to be signed and no visual aids, it is very unlikely that the solicitation will be completed at this meeting.

Remember, however, that this is not an "all or nothing" meeting; if the meeting place is not the one that you would choose, the next one may be more appropriate. It is not unusual for this to be merely the first of a series of such solicitation meetings before final agreement is reached, and these meetings might take place over a number of months or even years. Even a poor venue from your point of view is better than no meeting at all.

This is it! The time has come, and all the work leading up to this meeting is riding on how you undertake the gift solicitation. It can be a scary moment for many fundraisers, both professional and volunteer.

It shouldn't be, however. If the preparation has been done properly, then the solicitation itself can be the easiest thing in the world. The largest gift I ever solicited was achieved at a meeting that lasted barely 90 seconds.

How? Remember the phrase from the Introduction – *the right person asking the right person for the right thing at the right time for the right amount*. Before entering the room, therefore, one needs to check all of the following parameters:

The right person – is the person about to undertake the solicitation the right one? Does he or she know what to do, is he or she already known to the prospect, will he or she go into a blue funk and fail actually to ask for the gift?

Asking the right person – does the prospect actually have control of the funds and have access to the level of gift you are about to ask for, and is he or she suitably prepared through friend-raising and communications?

For the right thing – have you identified the project as one with which the prospect has an affinity?

At the right time – is this the right moment? Has the prospect's company just released terrible financial news? Has he or she just separated from a spouse? Did he or she get up on the wrong side of the bed this morning?

For the right amount – is the amount you are going to ask for justifiable? How does it relate to the project as a whole? Has the senior volunteer who is about to ask for this gift also given at a similar level?

Once the answers to these questions are known, then one can enter the room with confidence. In fact, at this stage, it is not at all unusual for the prospect to suggest, "Perhaps it's about time I did something" or to ask, "How can I help?" which is like knocking at an open door.

Continues on next page

As stated previously, the ideal person to be representing your interests in a solicitation meeting is a peer of the prospect who has donated personally at a substantial level. Even better is to have a pair of solicitors – the volunteer and a professional whose role is to facilitate who knows the various tax advantages of different giving methodologies, and who can dot the i's and cross the t's.

Only donors should ask, including professional fundraisers. It is reprehensible to expect a prospect to give to an individual who has not also made a gift.

If a peer of the prospect is not available, then it is still preferable to have two solicitors in the room. Preferably one should be the most senior representative of the organisation (perhaps the chief executive or chairman).

The fact remains, however, that far too many solicitations are undertaken by professional fundraisers alone. Although the best of them have got extremely good at it, it remains the second best option to having peers of the prospect "make the ask."

Successful solicitations tend to follow a fairly predictable pattern, as follows:

Small talk – it is very easy (because you are tense and excited about the major gift you are about to ask for) to launch into your "pitch" as soon as you have entered the room. Try and ease your way into the meeting by making conventional small talk: praise the house or the view, ask how the family is, question the current trading conditions for the prospect's business, or even comment on the ease (or lack of it) in reaching the meeting.

Listen – this introductory phase is very important in gauging the prospect's mood. If he or she is having a bad day, then this will become clear quite early on. Sometimes the first thing the individual wishes to tell you is that he or she has no intention of making a gift at this meeting, and you must pick this up immediately or risk embarrassment and a possible souring of the relationship. If the "vibes" you pick up are positive, then go forward.

The project – explain the project in detail. Show why it is important, how it will work, how the beneficiaries of your organisation will benefit, and ask for his or her views and opinions.

Listen – major donors like to be heavily involved in the projects they fund. They may have opinions on what you have outlined, and you need to be sure, if you ask for the gift, that you can agree on any changes or amendments the donor suggests. You also need to hear from the prospect's lips that he or she thinks the project is a good and worthwhile idea.

The "Ask" – the actual solicitation should be clear, calm and relatively short. The basic premise of your approach should be, given that he or she agrees with the plan or project, to ask if he or she would consider a gift of a specific sum of money to make it a reality. You must, in other words, specify exactly the size of gift you want.

Reviewer's Comment

I find that where the precise size of a hoped for gift is difficult to quantify, there is merit in specifying a narrow range rather than an exact amount.

The "silence" – probably the hardest thing to do when soliciting a major gift is to ask for the specific amount and then stay silent. This is vital, however. Many senior volunteers' ribs have been badly bruised by attendant fundraising directors' elbows jabbing repeatedly into their midriffs as they attempt to say something after the "ask." There is an almost overwhelming urge to "soften" the request and say, "But of course if that's too much, anything you choose to donate would be really appreciated." The longer the silence goes on, the more you feel the urge to moderate your demand and give the prospect a "get out" clause that he or she will invariably take.

Continues on next page

The decision – more often than not, what is going on in the prospect's mind during this silence is working out *how* the gift is going to be made and not *whether* it will be made. Wealthy people do not, as a rule, keep large amounts of cash sitting in bank accounts earning no interest. Their money works for them or is invested long term. Equally, many donors are creative in how they put large gifts together – some from family trusts, some from their businesses, some from their own resources – with one eye on tax-effectiveness in particular, and this needs to be worked out before a decision can be made.

Negotiations – it is not at all unusual for the answer, when it finally comes, to be conditional. This is when you need to be able to negotiate in confidence. If the donor wishes to have his or her name on the project, is that something you can promise? Can you assist the donor in reducing the net cost by showing him or her a tax-effective method of giving? Can you overcome potential objections by working with his or her accountant, making an appointment to explain the project to other members of the family, etc.?

Reviewer's Comment

The ability to "negotiate in confidence" is vital. The governing board should establish a policy of naming rights or recognition prior to major gift solicitation.

Closing – more money is lost through a failure to properly close a negotiated deal than for any other reason. It is as if, once the donor has agreed, a great weight is taken off the solicitors' shoulders, and, with profuse thanks, they scuttle out of the door. It is crucially important that you state very clearly and precisely back to the donor what you believe the agreement to be, when the money will be paid, what acknowledgments and public recognition will be granted, and what involvement the donor will have with the project itself. You then need to put this in writing as soon as you return to the office.

The amount you have asked for is, of course, crucial to the success of both your solicitation and the project for which you are seeking funding. You must be able to justify the amount to the prospect and show why it has to be the size it is. It must also be affordable by the prospect. But, equally, no one ever got angry for being requested too much, so when making your calculations, err on the side of generosity.

Feel free to make use of *tables of giving* to show why the gift should be the size you have asked for. Explain that a project that costs one million cannot be broken down into a thousand gifts of one thousand, that a lead gift such as you are asking for needs to be at least 25 percent of the total. Above all, if you are forced during the negotiation phase to reduce your request, do not, as so many do, come down in too large an increment. One million is too much? How about nine hundred thousand? Similarly, do not give away naming opportunities too cheaply. A gift of 10 percent of the total required should not, and must not, be enough to have the project named after the donor.

Finally, remember that a negative response is usually the result of bad research and/or preparation and that failure only truly exists if you have closed off all future approaches. Do not be afraid to not ask for the gift if the timing or the mood is wrong, and thank a prospect for his or her time and ideally make an appointment for a future meeting if the immediate answer is a negative one.

The proper stewardship of a donor is the first step to getting the next gift. Having gone to so much trouble to find, befriend, communicate with and solicit the prospect, it is crucially important that you maximise that effort by ensuring that the donor remains a friend and supporter.

The best way of ensuring that no major supporter slips through the stewardship net is to set down a stewardship policy that is understood and followed by all. This will include the following.

Options

Before solicitation begins for any project, it should be agreed by the board or governing body what acknowledgment vehicles are available to major donors – naming opportunities for all or part of the project, patron or benefactor status, an offer to join the board or development committee, etc. – and for how much.

Thanks

- Fundraising director telephones immediately to thank donor.

- Personal letter from fundraising director follows.

- Personal letter (drafted by fundraising director) is sent from chief executive.

- Handwritten note is sent from chairman of the board.

Public recognition

Before any recognition or public statements take place, the donor's preferences must be sought. Some may wish to remain anonymous.

On the basis that they are happy to be named, list and keep thanking your major donors in every conceivable publication.

Ensure the continued value of any naming opportunity – the donor is buying immortality by having something named after him or her. If, for example, you knock down a building paid for by a benefactor in 1925, you must ensure that whatever replaces it also memorialises that benefactor. Otherwise, current donors will not trust that their names, in turn, will continue to be memorialised.

Involvement

Some major donors will insist upon being heavily involved in the project they are funding; even if they do not insist upon this, it is important that you keep them personally abreast of developments. How are you getting on with recruiting the new staff they are paying for? Where are you with planning permission for the new building? Let them know.

There is nothing better than inviting the donor to see a building project during construction. There is something about putting a hard hat on and wandering over a building site in rubber boots which truly inspires donors.

Have an opening launch event for whatever sort of project the donor is funding and consider asking the donor to cut the ribbon or break the bottle of champagne or unveil the plaque.

Ongoing communication
If you were ever in any doubt, the major donor is now a VIP as far as you are concerned, and it is all the more important that he/she feels personally in touch and looked after in the future. So write the personal note to the major donor and attach it to the general information sheets and newsletters sent to everyone, address the envelopes by hand, send the birthday cards and Christmas cards. They are all important if you want to maintain the relationship and continue to benefit from the munificence of your new benefactor.

CONCLUSION

Every professional fundraiser should be aware of the Pareto Principle, otherwise known as the 80:20 rule. Eighty percent of an NPO's donations will come from the top 20 percent of its donors. For many years this has been a truism, but over the last 20 years it has changed somewhat, especially among those organisations that have embraced fundraising from wealthy individuals. In fact, in some places the ratio is over 90:10 and even higher.

The purpose of this interesting but, in practical terms, useless statistic is to encourage you to undertake this long, slow and arduous process with wealthy individuals because, at the end of the day, it is extraordinarily productive and can transform your fundraising performance.

There is only one guiding principle to remember throughout this whole process: How would you like to be treated in similar circumstances? If you genuinely care about the opinions and foibles of your wealthy individual prospects, then you will succeed. Think about them, nurture them, care about them and, above all, listen to them. They can bring far more than just their wealth to your cause.

■ A major donor will know many other major gift prospects whom he or she could solicit for you in due course.

■ He or she will have skills and experience that could greatly benefit your organisation.

■ He or she will have access to resources and information that you would never otherwise be able to exploit.

Preparation is the key. Research, connections, friend-raising, and the right person making the right approach lead to another old saying in the profession:

Fundraising is what happens when everything else has gone right!